NINJAS

Natalie Hyde

CRABTREE
Publishing Company
www.crabtreebooks.com

Crabtree Publishing Company
www.crabtreebooks.com

Author: Natalie Hyde
Publishing plan research and development: Reagan Miller
Editors: Rachel Minay, Kathy Middleton
Proofreader: Wendy Scavuzzo
Photo Researcher: Natalie Hyde/Rachel Minay
Original design: Tim Mayer (Mayer Media)
Book design: Clare Nicholas
Cover design: Ken Wright
Production coordinator and prepress tecnician: Ken Wright
Print coordinator: Katherine Berti

Produced for Crabtree Publishing Company by White-Thomson Publishing

Cover:
iStock: (center);
Shutterstock: Seita (background)

Photographs:
Alamy: AF archive: p. 43; LCM NW: p. 33; **Corbis:** Bloomimage: pp. 18–19; Colin Anderson/Blend Images: p. 9; **Dreamstime:** Andriy Petrenko: pp. 44–45; Dreamstimepoint: p. 14; Radu Razvan Gheorghe: pp. 7, 15; Sean Pavone: pp. 6–7; **Shutterstock:** Anton Todorov: p. 21; cowardlion: p. 8; IZO: pp. 3, 28; Danomyte: p. 37; del.Monaco: p. 12; Dr_Flash pp. 38–39; Dynamicfoto: p. 23; Emir Simsek: p. 17; Fokin Oleg: p. 29; Fotokvadrat: pp. 4–5; Number001: p. 21; redstone: p. 35; RoidRanger: p. 42; rudall30: pp. 10–11; Santia: p. 16; Slavoljub Pantelic: p. 38; Stephen Coburn: p. 40; steve estvanik: p. 32; Tooykrub: p. 25; Volodymyr Krasyuk: p. 39; Yuriy Chertok: p. 20; **Thinkstock:** estelle hood: p. 36; fukuyama1015: pp. 12–13; RossellaApostoli: p. 1; **Topfoto:** The Granger Collection: pp. 26–27; **Wikimedia:** : pp. 22, 24, 30, 34; Qurren (talk): p. 31; Shadowleafcutlery: p. 41.

Library and Archives Canada Cataloguing in Publication

Hyde, Natalie, 1963-, author
   Ninjas / Natalie Hyde.

(Crabtree chrome)
Includes index.
Issued in print and electronic formats.
ISBN 978-0-7787-1365-4 (bound).--ISBN 978-0-7787-1401-9 (pbk.).--ISBN 978-1-4271-8980-6 (pdf).--ISBN 978-1-4271-8974-5 (html)

   1. Ninja--Juvenile literature. 2. Ninjutsu--Juvenile literature.
I. Title. II. Series: Crabtree chrome

UB271.J3H93 2014   j355.5'48   C2014-903915-8
                                          C2014-903916-6

Library of Congress Cataloging-in-Publication Data

Hyde, Natalie, 1963-
 Ninjas / Natalie Hyde.
      pages cm. -- (Crabtree chrome)
   Includes index.
  ISBN 978-0-7787-1365-4 (reinforced library binding) --
 ISBN 978-0-7787-1401-9 (pbk.) --
 ISBN 978-1-4271-8980-6 (electronic pdf) --
 ISBN 978-1-4271-8974-5 (electronic html)
 1. Ninja--Juvenile literature. I. Title.

 UB271.J3H93 2015
 355.5'48--dc23
                                          2014022782

Crabtree Publishing Company
www.crabtreebooks.com   1-800-387-7650   Printed in the U.S.A./092014/JA20140811

Published in Canada
Crabtree Publishing
616 Welland Ave.
St. Catharines, ON
L2M 5V6

Published in the United States
Crabtree Publishing
PMB 59051
350 Fifth Avenue, 59th Floor
New York, New York 10118

Published in the United Kingdom
Crabtree Publishing
Maritime House
Basin Road North, Hove
BN41 1WR

Published in Australia
Crabtree Publishing
3 Charles Street
Coburg North
VIC 3058

Contents

Japanese Secret Agents   4

Ninja Skills   16

Ninja Missions   22

Legendary Ninjas   30

Will the Real Ninja
  Please Stand Up?   36

Ninjas Today   42

Learning More   46

Glossary   47

Index   48

Japanese Secret Agents

Moving Shadows

Arakawa Shichirobci moved outside Hara Castle without making a sound. He set explosives and signaled to Mochizuki Yoemon. The men waited for the blast to **distract** the guards, then they could climb the castle walls. They were dressed like soldiers so, once they were inside, no one would suspect them.

Mission Accomplished!

Their job was to gather information on the enemy. They saw the enemy were low on food and weapons. Arakawa grabbed a castle banner as proof they had made it inside. Suddenly, they were noticed. They made their escape down the castle walls with gunfire all around them.

◀ *Ninjas often worked at night, when they were well hidden by the dark and guards were tired.*

Both Arakawa and Mochizuki were wounded. But the detailed plans of the castle and the secret passwords they discovered helped the shogun, or military leader, of the Tokugawa region, win the battle against the rebellious peasants.

distract: draw attention away from something

Who Were the Ninjas?

Ninjas were the secret agents of **medieval** Japan.
They were known for their amazing spying skills.
They could climb steep walls and leap over
huge gaps without getting hurt. They were
so good at sneaking in and out of
buildings that people thought
they had magic powers.

▶ *Japanese castles were built
mostly of wood. Ninjas often
used fire and explosives.
This meant castles were in
danger of burning
down during attacks.*

Some rulers were so afraid of
ninjas sneaking in at night
that they built "nightingale
floors." The floorboards in Nijo
Castle, Kyoto, chirped when
anyone stepped on them.

Hide in Plain Sight

Powerful rulers hired ninjas to help protect their
territories. Enemies were always trying to attack to
gain land. Ninjas gathered information on these
enemies by pretending to be peasants, musicians,
or even enemy soldiers. They were
masters of disguise.

▶ *A ninja might use
a monk disguise. The
large straw hat helped
hide the ninja's face.*

medieval: a time when Japan was ruled by powerful families

Who's in Charge?

In the 1300s, Japan was governed under the **feudal system**. The emperor was Japan's leader, but he did not hold real power. The country was divided into regions. The heads of powerful families, called daimyos, controlled these areas, along with the shogun, who was the head of the local army. The daimyos and the shoguns were the real rulers.

▶ *The title of shogun was usually passed from father to son.*

To Serve and Protect

The daimyo's army was made up of four kinds of warriors. The samurai were skilled fighters who were very loyal to their masters. Ashigaru were peasants who became regular soldiers. Ninjas were used to gather information. Warrior monks fought to protect the religious temples in the region.

▶ *Samurai armor was made for easy movement on the battlefield.*

A rōnin was a samurai without a master. Rōnin were looked down on by other samurai because a samurai was expected to kill himself if he lost his master.

feudal system: a system in which land is given for military service

Bushido and Ninjutsu

Samurai followed a strict code of **conduct** called bushido (the way of the warrior). They believed in fighting face to face, and hiding nothing. Ninjas, on the other hand, followed ninjutsu (see page 16). They were trained to hide, to pretend to be other people, and to tell no one what they were doing.

▶ *Bushido meant a true warrior showed loyalty, bravery, honor, and respect for life.*

A Bad Reputation

Ninjas were so secretive that no one was sure who they were or what they were up to. This made them both hated and feared. Most samurai disliked the ninjas' ways, but accepted that they were necessary. The information gathered by ninjas could help win a war.

In Japan, ninjas are referred to as *shinobi*. This means "to steal away." The aim of the shinobi was to make sure no one knew of their existence.

conduct: the way someone behaves

Home of the Ninjas

The Iga and Koga regions in Japan are known as the birthplace of the ninja. Legend says that a samurai met a Chinese monk traveling in the area. The samurai was unhappy with bushido, and the monk knew different fighting ways. Together they created ninjutsu.

▼ *Villages surrounded by mountains are easier to protect. There are usually only a few routes to guard against attacks.*

Houses where ninjas lived and trained had hidden stairways, hiding spaces in the floor, secret doors to hidden rooms, and escape tunnels.

Life in the Hills

Iga and Koga share a common border. The mountains surrounding these two areas separated and protected them from the rest of Japan. The people there created their own style of government. Instead of a daimyo, or one powerful family, they had groups of families called **clans** that were protected by the ninjas.

▲ *The Iga region was not an easy place to live. The sloped hills were difficult to farm, and crops had to be grown on terraces built by farmers..*

clans: groups of related families

Kunoichi

Unlike samurai, girls and women could train to be ninjas. Female ninjas are called kunoichi. They played an important role. In Japan's strict society, women could go places where men could not. Kunoichi disguised themselves as temple maidens, housekeepers, and dancers. They collected information from inside temples, castles, and the homes of officials.

▶ *In battles, kunoichi were just as deadly and well trained as shinobi.*

Mochizuki Chiyome was the wife of a samurai from the Koga region. After he died in 1575, she began to train orphaned and abandoned girls to become kunoichi.

Deadly Flowers

Their training was called *kunoichijutsu*, which means "the art of the deadly flower." Kunoichi received the same weapons training as men. They were also trained in dance and music to be able to blend in with performers. When ordered to **assassinate** an enemy, they usually used poison or a steel fan.

▶ *Dancing costumes could hide daggers or poisoned metal claws.*

assassinate: to murder someone in a surprise attack

Ninja Skills

What Is Ninjutsu?

Ninjutsu is not a martial art or training as an assassin. It is the art of **espionage**. Besides fighting, hiding, leaping, and running, ninjas also learned to study the weather, the stars, the landscape, and their enemy's mind.

▼ *Studying the stars and the sky helped ninjas travel at night without maps.*

Four Main Goals

There are four main goals of ninjutsu. Ninjas had to be able to survive in the wild, get into forbidden places, move about without being seen, and deal with stress with a brave heart. These skills helped them to survive in dangerous times.

▼ *Ninjas needed to be ready to fight inside or outside and at any time of day.*

Because of their abilities to move around unseen, some people claimed ninjas had magical powers. They believed ninjas could walk on water and make themselves invisible.

espionage: spying to get information

What Are "the 18 Skills"?

Ninjas had to master 18 ninjutsu skills. These included weapon skills such as sword **techniques**, using throwing weapons, and working with explosives. Other skills deal with disguises, water training, escaping, and horse riding. The 18 skills helped ninjas to face any situation.

"[Ninjutsu is] to know and accept one's fate, and to live for human beings and all other creatures. The person who masters all of these is a ninja."

Masaaki Hatsumi

▼ *Ninjas were experts at using their environment to hide.*

Ninjas Versus Samurai

Samurai warriors also learned the 18 skills. The difference was in how the skills were used. Ninjas had to adapt them for surprise attacks and ambushes. They often had to use their skills in small spaces, such as hallways or doorways, or in the dark.

techniques: ways of doing something

Ninja Weapons

Ninjas needed weapons that they could easily hide or carry while running and climbing. The o-wakazashi sword was short and light. Shuriken were metal rings and stars. They were thrown at an attacker as a distraction. Ninjas also used finger rings with spikes and **sickles** with chains.

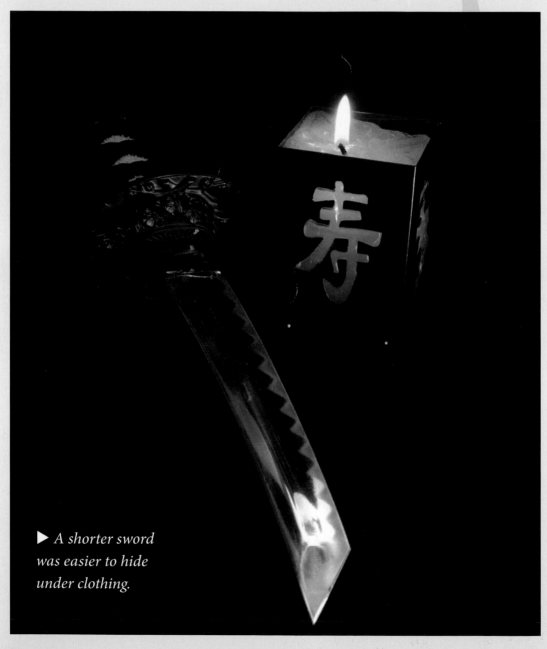

▶ *A shorter sword was easier to hide under clothing.*

Tools of the Trade

Ninjas used hooks attached to ropes to help them scale walls. Crowbars and folding saws were used to break into buildings. When not in disguise, a ninja might wear loose pants and a jacket called a shinobi shozuku. This outfit was usually dark blue to blend in with the night sky.

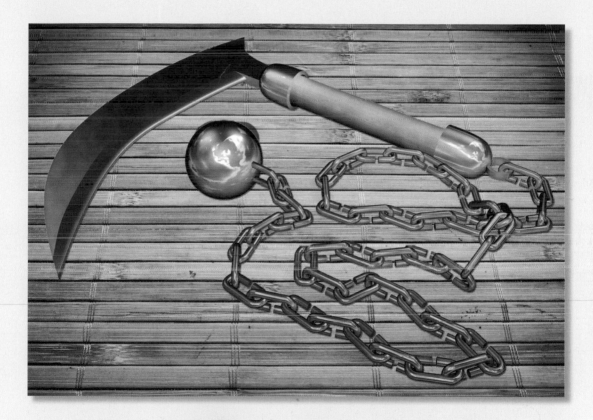

▲ *A ninja threw the heavy ball end first to tangle the enemy's weapons or arms before attacking him with the sickle.*

Ninjas used a listening device called a saoto hikigane. It looked like a metal cone. With it, they could hear faint sounds and listen in on nearby conversations.

sickles: farming tools with short handles and curved blades

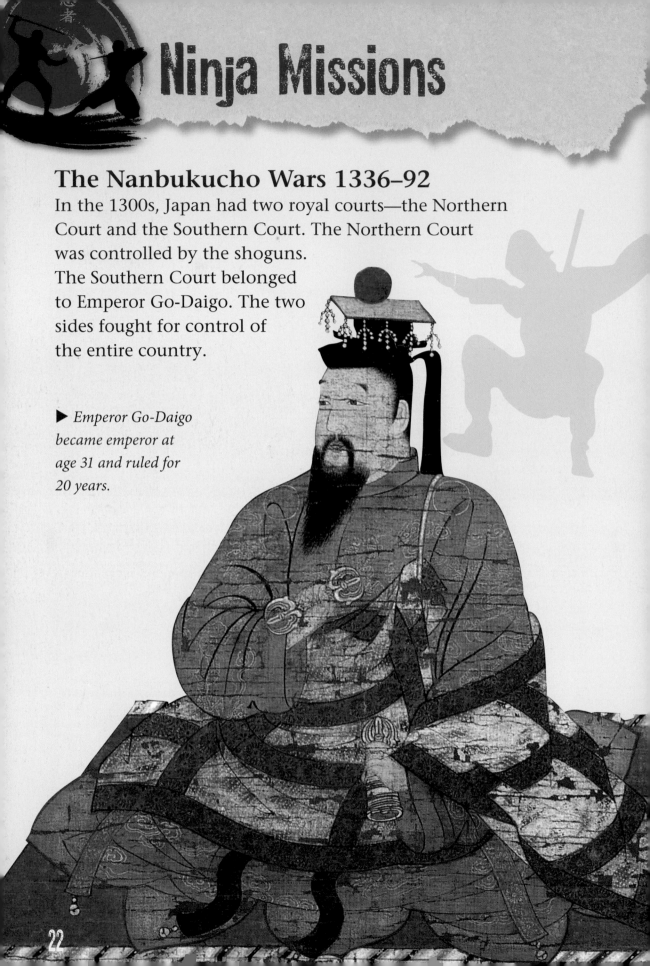

Ninja Missions

The Nanbukucho Wars 1336–92

In the 1300s, Japan had two royal courts—the Northern Court and the Southern Court. The Northern Court was controlled by the shoguns. The Southern Court belonged to Emperor Go-Daigo. The two sides fought for control of the entire country.

▶ *Emperor Go-Daigo became emperor at age 31 and ruled for 20 years.*

North and South

Both sides turned to the ninjas for help. They used them to spy on each other and gather information about troops and supplies. Ninjas from the North even burned down the South's Hachiman-yama Fortress. The Northern Court won in the end.

◀ *Fire distracted enemies, so ninjas could sneak into buildings.*

Ninjas were experts with explosives and fire. They used it for distraction, **arson**, and for signaling.

arson: to set something on fire on purpose

The Ōnin War 1467–77

The Ōnin War started as a fight among members of the Ashikaga clan over who would rule. It soon spread to the whole country. The war ended without a clear winner. This marked the start of the Sengoku Period, or "Warring States Period" (1467–1615), in which samurai clans continued to fight each other. It was during this period that the ninjas reached the height of their power.

▼ *This picture is of Ashikaga Yoshihisa. His fight to take power from his brother began the Ōnin War.*

Spies and Scouts

During this time, clans hired ninjas to help them gain control over territory. Ninjas acted as spies and scouts. They also worked as **agitators** and surprise attackers. They distracted the defenders with explosives and fires while the main army attacked the castle.

▼ *Ninjas were experts at setting and timing explosions.*

Often the first ninja to get inside a target wrote his name on the wall. That way, he got credit when his commander entered.

agitators: people who urge others to protest or rebel

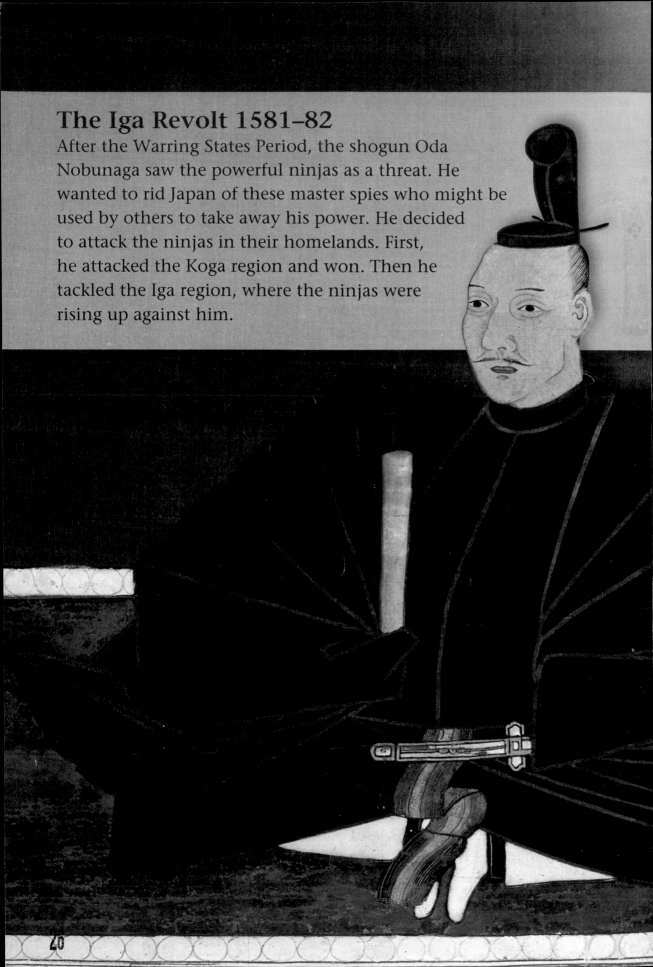

The Iga Revolt 1581–82

After the Warring States Period, the shogun Oda
Nobunaga saw the powerful ninjas as a threat. He
wanted to rid Japan of these master spies who might be
used by others to take away his power. He decided
to attack the ninjas in their homelands. First,
he attacked the Koga region and won. Then he
tackled the Iga region, where the ninjas were
rising up against him.

Stand and Fight

Nobunaga marched on the Iga region with 40,000 men. They attacked from six directions at once. The surprise attack caught the ninjas off guard. They did not have time to plan distractions or raids. They were forced to fight battles in the open. Thousands of ninjas died. The rest escaped into the mountains.

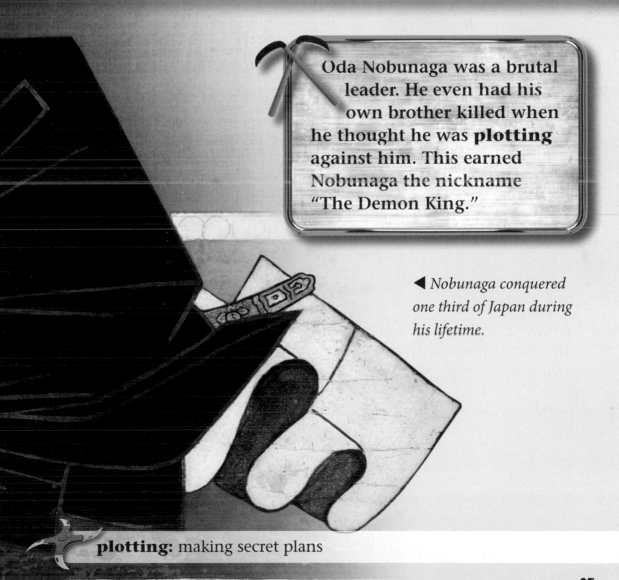

Oda Nobunaga was a brutal leader. He even had his own brother killed when he thought he was **plotting** against him. This earned Nobunaga the nickname "The Demon King."

◀ *Nobunaga conquered one third of Japan during his lifetime.*

plotting: making secret plans

Shimabara Rebellion 1637–38

The era of ninjas faded with the beginning of the Edo Period in 1603. The Shimabara Rebellion was the last time ninjas played a major role in a battle. The shogun in the Tokugawa region raised the peasants' taxes. He needed to pay for a new castle in Shimabara. He also wanted to get rid of the Christians in the area. Peasants and Christians both **revolted**.

▼ *Shimabara Castle was burned to the ground after the rebellion. A new one was rebuilt in 1964.*

Even though the ninjas knew there was a good chance they would die during the mission, many agreed to help the shogun.

Months of Fighting

In response, the shogun sent in 125,000 troops. The final battle was at Hara Castle. It lasted many months. Both sides suffered losses. The ninjas gave the shogun vital information. He knew the enemy was running out of supplies. He attacked and defeated them.

▲ *The rebels were low on food. They survived by scraping seaweed from rocks near the castle at low tide.*

 revolted: tried to overthrow a ruler

Legendary Ninjas

Prince Ōsu (Yamato Takeru)

Japanese legends are the first stories to describe ninja **behavior**. The tale of Prince Ōsu is one of the earliest. As a young man, he killed his brother in a rage. The emperor was afraid of his temper. He sent Prince Ōsu far away to fight their enemies.

▼ *One of Prince Ōsu's enemies was impressed by his bravery. He gave him the nickname Yamato Takeru, which means "The Brave of Yamato (region)."*

The sword that Prince Ōsu used in his legendary deeds is said to actually exist, but it is guarded so closely that no one has seen it in centuries.

Who Is That Woman?

Prince Ōsu used the ninja skill of disguise to survive.
He was invited to a dinner party by one of his father's
enemies. Prince Ōsu put on a woman's robe and makeup.
His enemy was completely fooled. He let the ninja prince
get close to him and Prince Ōsu stabbed him.

▼ *The Atsuta Shrine houses over 4,000 sacred
items, including Prince Ōsu's sword.*

 behavior: the way someone acts

Legend of Kumawaka

A monk was holding 13-year-old Kumawaka's father prisoner. When Kumawaka heard that his father was dying, he was desperate to see him. The monk refused. Kumawaka never saw his father again. He wanted revenge on the monk.

◄ The monk was called Homma. Another monk later helped Kumawaka by carrying the boy on his back so he would not leave footprints.

Spying in the Night

Kumawaka knew he wasn't strong enough to fight Homma. Instead, he pretended to be sick so the monk would take him in. At night, he would sneak around to learn where everyone slept and where the guards were. Finally, one night, he snuck in and stabbed Homma as revenge.

> "Kumawaka took his way in **stealth** to Homma's sleeping apartment, thinking, 'This assuredly is the good fortune I have awaited!'"
>
> *The Taiheiki Chronicle*

▲ *After the murder, Kumawaka used a bamboo tree to drop to the other side of the river and make his escape.*

stealth: careful and secret movement

Jiraiya

Ninjas also appear in Japanese folktales. One tale tells the story of Jiraiya, who was a ninja that used **shapeshifting** magic. He turned himself into a giant toad and fell in love with a beautiful young girl. She too had magic powers and turned herself into a slug.

▼ *The story of Jiraiya has been told in novels, plays, movies, and video games.*

The Evil Serpent

But the couple's life together was not always smooth. An evil ninja, named Orochimaru, used shapeshifting to turn into a giant snake. He attacked them. They tried to poison him but failed. Luckily, a student of Jiraiya's came along and saved him and the girl.

▲ *Snakes were often seen as villains in Japanese folktales because they could use poison to harm people.*

Many people thought ninjas practiced magic. They did practice *kuji*, which means "nine syllables." These were hand movements and chants used to strengthen their spirit.

shapeshifting: being able to change your shape, size, and looks

Will the Real Ninja Please Stand Up?

Black Masks?

Myth: Ninjas wore black clothing and masks.

Truth: Most of the time ninjas wore a disguise and not black clothing. They needed to blend in with their enemy, not stand out. The black outfit we see in films and pictures comes from costumes used in Japanese theater.

▶ *Monks wore sandals made from straw rope.*

Ninjas often dressed as monks. The loose robes let them hide weapons. Monks were also allowed to go in and out of buildings easily.

Weapons

Myth: Ninjas had special swords and weapons.

Truth: Most ninjas were spies. Most swords and weapons would be too **noticeable**. If they needed to fight, they often used farm tools such as sickles. These didn't look like weapons if they were seen.

▲ *When people think of ninjas, they think of an attacker in a black costume and mask.*

noticeable: easily seen

Shuriken

Myth: Shuriken were "throwing stars" meant to kill.
Truth: A shuriken was any tool that could be thrown with the hand. This included knives, **discs**, and metal rings. They were mostly used to distract enemies, not kill them.

▼ *The art of throwing a shuriken is called shurikenjutsu.*

Some shuriken were not even thrown. They were placed in the ground with their blade pointing up. Some had poison on them. This would cut an enemy's feet and make them ill or even kill them.

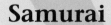

Samurai

Myth: Samurai and ninjas worked against each other.
Truth: Many ninjas came from the samurai class. They also received the same training. Both knew that the other was important to win a battle. Some were even a samurai by day and a ninja by night.

▶ *Samurai relied on the information brought by ninjas to win battles.*

discs: flat, thin, round objects

Could Ninjas Fly?

Myth: Ninjas could fly, disappear into thin air, and walk on water.

Truth: Some reports say Ninjas used a cape with a stick to hang-glide when jumping long distances. They also shaped bamboo into a type of snowshoe to help them cross water without sinking.

▶ *As time went on, legends about the abilities of ninjas grew.*

Most myths about **supernatural** powers were started by the ninjas themselves. This would help to make others afraid of them.

Could Ninjas Shapeshift?

Myth: Ninjas were able to shapeshift.
Truth: Sometimes ninjas used claws on their
hands and spikes on their feet to climb better.
This made their tracks look like an animal's.

▲ *A ninja using hand claws could climb a tree like a
bear or a cat. People who saw the tracks of the claws
might think the ninja had shapeshifted into a beast.*

supernatural: not explained by science or the laws of nature

Ninjas Today

Where Are All the Historical Records?

There are not many records of ninjas. Their purpose was to be secret. Ancient writers may have avoided mentioning them. Sneaking around was not considered honorable. If ninjas are mentioned in historical writings, it is likely because their work was very important.

▼ *American Ninja Warrior is a TV competition in which people race through an obstacle course.*

The Popular Ninja

The work of ninjas was made more popular because of Japanese theater. Plays **exaggerated** their skills and mysterious ways. People began to think all ninjas wore black masks and assassinated people. Films still often show ninjas in this way.

▲ *The Teenage Mutant Ninja Turtles are characters from comics and TV shows. They are heroes trained in the art of ninjutsu.*

The first major appearance of ninjas in Western culture was in the James Bond film *You Only Live Twice*, with a secret commando force of the Japanese intelligence service.

 exaggerated: made something sound bigger or better than it really is

The End of the Ninjas

The Edo Period (1603–1868) brought peace to Japan. There were no large **civil wars** or major battles. The ninjas' skills were no longer needed. Some ninjas may have found new work as palace guards.

▶ *There are martial arts schools for students of all ages.*

There are still martial arts schools that teach ninjutsu-style skills. Most have adapted training to fit with our modern culture.

Are There Any Ninjas Today?

Jinichi Kawakami is from the historic
Iga region. He is the head of the
Koka clan. He hasn't named
anyone to continue as leader.
He doesn't think ninjas'
skills are as important in
the modern world.

Ninja Timeline

1162	Daisuke Togakure meets the Chinese monk Kain Doshi. Together they develop ninjutsu.
1336–92	The ninjas work as spies as the Northern Court and Southern Court battle in the Nanbukucho Wars.
1467	Ninjas provide information as civil war breaks out across Japan in the Onin War.
1467–1615	During the Sengoku Period ("Warring States Period"), ninjas are used during the endless fighting over land and power.
1581	Oda Nobunaga attacks the Iga area with 40,000 men to defeat the ninjas.
1603–1868	Japan enjoys peaceful times and the ninja ways slowly disappear.

civil wars: wars fought between people in the same country

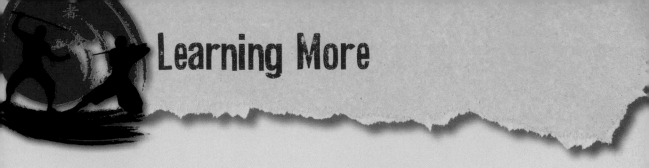

Learning More

Books

Life as a Ninja
by Matt Doeden
(Capstone Press, 2010)

Ninja (Warriors of History)
by Jason Glaser
(Edge Books, 2006)

Ninja (Fierce Fighters)
by Charlotte Guillain
(Raintree, 2011)

Ninjas (Great Warriors)
by Carla Mooney
(ABDO, 2013)

*Ninjas: Masters of Stealth
and Secrecy* (Way of the
Warrior)
by Joanne Mattern
(Children's Press, 2005)

Real Ninja
by Coral Tulloch
(Enchanted Lion Books, 2008)

Websites

www.winjutsu.com/
ninjakids/
History and stories at
Ninja Kids

www.youtube.com/
watch?v=MMM3hVp-1Ag
This Lost History video looks at
ninja lore

www.kallikids.com/en/
KalliKids/For-families/expert-
pin-boards/index.cfm/page/
ninjutsu
Facts and tips for kids
interested in learning ninjutsu

Glossary

agitators People who urge others to protest or rebel

arson To set something on fire on purpose

assassinate To murder someone in a surprise attack

behavior The way someone acts

civil wars Wars fought between people in the same country

clans Groups of related families

conduct The way someone behaves

discs Flat, thin, round objects

distract Draw attention away from something

espionage Spying to get information

exaggerated Made something sound bigger or better than it really is

feudal system A system in which land is given for military service

medieval A time when Japan was ruled by powerful families

noticeable Easily seen

plotting Making secret plans

revolted Tried to overthrow a ruler

shapeshifting Being able to change your shape, size, and looks

sickles Farming tools with short handles and curved blades

stealth Careful and secret movement

supernatural Not explained by science or the laws of nature

techniques Ways of doing something

Index

Entries in **bold** refer to pictures

18 skills 18, 19

American Ninja Warrior **42**
Arakawa Shichirobei 4, 5
ashigaru 9
Ashikaga Yoshihisa **24**

Buddhists 5
bushido 10, 12

castles 4, 5, **6**, 14, 25, 28, 29
Christians 5, 28
clans 13, 24, 25, 45
clothing 20, 36

daimyos 8, 9, 13
disguises **7**, 14, 18, 31, 36

Edo Period 28, 44
emperors 8, 22, 30
explosives 4, 6, 18, 23, 25

feudal system 8
fire 6, 23, **23**, 25

Go-Daigo, Emperor 22, **22**

Hara Castle 4, 29

Iga 12, **12–13**, 13, 26, 27, 45
Iga Revolt 26–27

Jiraiya 34, **34**, 35

Koga 12, 13, 14, 26
kuji 35
Kumawaka 32, 33, **33**
kunoichi 14, **14**, 15

legends 12, 30–35, 40

magic 6, 17, 34, 35
Mochizuki Chiyome 14
Mochizuki Yoemon 4, 5
monks 7, 9, 12, 32, **32**, 33, 36, **36**, 45
myths 36–41

Nanbukucho Wars 22–23, 45
ninjutsu 10, 12, 16, 17, 18, 43, 44, 45

Oda Nobunaga 26, **26–27**, 27, 45
Ōnin War 24, 45
Ōsu, Prince 30, **30**, 31

rōnin 9

samurai 9, **9**, 10, 11, 12, 14, 19, 24, 39, **39**
Sengoku Period 24, 26, 45
shapeshifting 34, 35, 41
Shimabara Castle **28**
Shimabara Rebellion 28–29
shoguns 8, **8**, 22, 26, 28, 29
shuriken 20, 38, **38**
sickles 20, **21**, 37
skills 6, 16–21, 31, 43, 44, 45
snakes 35, **35**
swords 20, **20**, 30, 31, 37

Teenage Mutant Ninja Turtles **43**

Warring States Period 24, 26, 45
weapons 5, 15, 18, 20, 21, 36, 37

Yamato Takeru 30, **30**, 31